WHAT ONCE WAS

"Omphalos (Allegory of Happiness)" – Elaine Amyot

WHAT ONCE WAS

EDWARD LEMOND

FOREWORD BY
ELIZABETH BLANCHARD

CHAPEL STREET EDITIONS

Copyright © 2019 by Edward Lemond

All rights reserved

Published by
Chapel Street Editions
150 Chapel Street
Woodstock, New Brunswick E7M 1H4
www.chapelstreeteditions.com

ISBN 978-1-988299-28-0

Library and Archives Canada Cataloguing in Publication

Title: What once was / Edward Lemond ; foreword by Elizabeth Blanchard
Names: Lemond, Edward, 1942- author. | Blanchard, Elizabeth, 1961- writer of foreword.
Description: Poems.
Identifiers: Canadiana 20200154702 | ISBN 9781988299280 (softcover)
Classification: LCC PS8623.E548 W53 2020 | DDC C811/.6—dc23

Cover artwork: "Male Mothering" by Elaine Amyot
Frontispiece: "Omphalos (Allegory of Happiness)" by Elaine Amyot
Page 120: "Renewal" by Elaine Amyot

Book design by Brendan Helmuth

Dedication

This book is dedicated to the memory of my wife,
Elaine Amyot.

CONTENTS

Foreword i
Preface v
What Once Was 1
   Things Happen 2
   Her Own Way 4
   The Word 6
   The Forest in Ruins 8
   Overextended 12
   Before the Earth Froze 14
   No Beginning, No End 16
   White Noise 18
   Sleep, My Love 20
   Ally 22
   Cloud of Forgetting 24
   Fat, Wet Flakes 26
   The Mental Life of Plants and Worms 28
   The Days Grow Longer 32
   Real Life 34
   What I Wanted To Say 36
   These Various Proofs 38
   I Can't Say I'm Sorry 42
   A Fighting Chance 44
   The Art of Camouflage 46
   Ode to Ice 48
   The Last Thing She Wants 50
   Ode to Hands 52
   Perhaps 54
   Her Smile 56
   Chance Stars 58

A Mistake	60
Don't Even Ask	62
Strangers in the Night	64
Ode to Cats	66
It's All Right	68
She Continues	70
Ode to Bodies	72
Standing Here at the Cutting Board	74
What Once Was	76
Ode to Laughter	78
Ode to Neighbors	80
The Bumblebee	84
Everywhere He Goes	86
Low Tide	88
It's Later Than You Think	90
Hot and Humid	92
She's Busy Now	94
Then Let It Go	96
Weeds, and More Weeds	98
Too Bad for Them	100
Ode to Hiding Places	102
When She Talks Like That	104
Be Joyful	106
Uncoupling/Coupling	108
Ode to Dragonflies	110
A New Shirt	112
Acknowledgments	115
About the Author	119
About the Artist	121

FOREWORD

In *What Once Was*, Edward Lemond writes from the claustrophobic corridor of terminal illness, that narrow passage travelled by those who suffer an illness to its end, be it the one leaving, or the one to be left behind. It's the painful yet privileged intimacy of this space that renders this collection of poetry so compelling—a series of poems Ed wrote over a 12-month period when caring for his wife and friend, Elaine Amyot, in the final 18 months of her life.

The notion of constriction, which is articulated by the speaker in the very first poem—"because life seems to be giving them / fewer and fewer choices"—is very much present throughout the book. It's expressed in the narrowing of physical space, "to keep moving, if only around / the house, from room to room"; in the restriction of movement, "Her body, once active, / has begun to break down"; in the decrease of social interactions, "All my friends have forgotten me." Even the psychological space is limited to the point where "An afternoon rest, / … is a kind of / hiding place," and dreams must be abandoned if one is "to go on living" life, as though the mind no longer has enough stretch to encompass both the real and the imagined. Illness binds body and spirit, but "Worst of all / is the feeling of isolation."

The depth of the isolation expressed by the poet is better understood in light of the fullness of the couple's life prior to Elaine's illness. Ed and Elaine came together later in life. They met in Moncton at a café on Main Street on a warm afternoon in July. Elaine was a well-known visual artist and a retired teacher, a francophone from Quebec who had settled in Acadie years earlier. Ed, an American-born bookseller and writer, was new to the city. Having recently sold his business in Halifax, he had just leased space for the bookstore he planned to open in Moncton.

They were married a year later. I remember the year not because I attended the wedding, but because it was the year my son was born, 1994. I would only come to know the couple when I moved to the area in 1999. I began attending the Attic Owl readings, a monthly reading series that Ed founded and hosted in his bookstore of the same name, a reading series that continues to welcome authors from across the country to this day.

Eventually, Elaine would invite me to write essays for her upcoming exhibitions. We were all members of the same writers group, the Breach House Gang. I, like many others, grew to admire the couple's tireless efforts to promote the literary and visual arts in the community they had adopted, and which had adopted them. Friends knew them as Ed and Elaine. Rarely was one mentioned without the other, an unconscious response to the couple's complicity in all things.

The singular kinship they shared animates Ed's poetry. It can be felt in the speaker's unremitting and focused attention on "her": the partner, the one who is ill. The poetic voice is that of a loved one, a caretaker, a companion who possesses intimate knowledge of "her" activities, "her" thoughts, "her" feelings. At times, so close is the speaker to the object of his devotion, the "her" disappears into an indistinguishable "I." In the poem "The Days Grow Longer," it isn't clear to whom the "I" refers. It's as if the two have been compressed into a single space where emotional boundaries dissolve and the vulnerability of illness infects all:

"... For the first time
in my life I would like to go south
for the winter. Trees know
when one of their kind is sick,
don't ask me how. Sometimes

the tallest, strongest-looking tree
is the one that falls ... "

This particular poem was written in the final days of the calendar year. We know this because every poem in the collection is dated. In doing so, the author affords a temporal structure to the work, adds a chronological perspective to the lens through which the collection is viewed. Knowing when one poem was written in relation to the other invites comparison, draws attention to the shifting of emotions across poems.

A series of discrete reflections becomes a journey. There is a sense of movement, of progressing through the illness with the speaker. The date also anchors each poem to the time of the year it was written, imbuing the text with seasonal symbolism. "The Days Grow Longer" was penned deep in December, at a time when sunlight fades early and the nights are long. The thought of a cold and dark landscape weighs heavy on the psyche, impresses upon the mind how deeply is felt the suffering of a loved one.

Elaine passed away on February 27, 2019, five months after Ed completed this collection of poetry. I attended the funeral. My son would turn 25 a month later. Theirs was a shared journey of a quarter-century. In one of the final poems in the book, the speaker imagines the life cycle of a dragonfly, the liberating metamorphosis of the insect freed from the confines of the nymph's cocoon. It speaks of "the transformation of death / into something that can be accepted, even welcomed." Elaine, who had a profound love of nature, must have liked this image. She believed the ancientness of the earth pointed to the eternal in all of us. I am reminded of the words of Emily Brontë's poem "No Coward Soul Is Mine." Perhaps so narrowed is the passage at the end of the journey, "There is not room for Death."

Elizabeth Blanchard

PREFACE

September 18, 2013. My wife and I drove from our house in Dieppe, New Brunswick to nearby Sackville, to walk in the Waterfowl Park and have a cup of coffee at an outdoor café. Returning along Main Street to the parking lot where we'd left the car, I became fascinated with Douglas Lochhead's series of poems that had been attached to power poles along the way, one for each day of the month of September. They were short poems about the Tantramar Marsh – descriptive, meditative, reflective, impressionistic. I'd like to do something like this, I said to myself.

At home, I wrote the first, titled September 19. The next day I wrote another, titled September 20. A line from the German poet Rilke's "Requiem For a Friend," in the Stephen Mitchell translation, echoed in my head: "You had just one desire: a years-long work." So I leap-frogged to the notion that I would do this for one year, from September 19, 2013 to September 19, 2014. That's the journey I embarked upon, and carried through to completion, as I had promised myself, though toward the end the challenge of making a new, well-formed poem each and every day became daunting.

Jump forward three years, to September 22, 2017, when I found myself rejuvenated and ready to challenge myself again. One poem a day for one year had given me some poetic high moments. One poem a day for one year, however, was a burden too heavy once again to carry, and so I settled on one poem a week for one year, which allowed the poems to be more open-ended, more fulsome, and instead of letting various themes emerge unbidden from the darkness of the unconscious, I chose to stay as nearly as possible to the one theme that mattered most to me at this time, the theme of a man and a woman growing into old age together, struggling with its afflictions, finding what comfort they can in themselves and in the beauty and unstoppable life force of the natural world. The cycle would reflect the changing seasons, moods, challenges, whatever struck me most forcefully during a particular week.

The woman, modeled on my wife, visual artist Elaine Amyot, though not exactly identical to her, suffers from congestive heart failure, a long-lasting, progressive disease, which kills by a thousand cuts. During the writing of these poems, up to September 14, 2018, Elaine was still active and able to get out and do things. But a month or two later she became housebound because of lack of stamina, lack of breath, and on February 27, 2019, she died in hospital, in the embrace of family and friends.

Edward Lemond

WHAT ONCE WAS

THINGS HAPPEN

He dips deeply into the dish,
turns his hand over several times.
An even number means he gets
the first crack, an odd number means

she does. It is a game they play
because life seems to be giving them
fewer and fewer choices, and even those
have become increasingly pointless,
save for the one that nags,

whether to live or to die, that is
always there, in the back of their minds.
Who needs who, and who can get along
just fine by himself, everybody knows.
Sometimes he likes to stay home,

sometimes she does too, though not
as often. If it rains or snows,
they might agree what to do,
or they might not. It's hard
to tell. They have such different ideas.

But if there is one thing they see
eye to eye on it is the need
never to equivocate. Make a decision
and stick to it, otherwise
what's the point?

Sure, things happen,
and you can either let them
get you down, or you can deal with them,
like the turning of the seasons.

(September 22)

HER OWN WAY

Her coat streaked with rain,
her shoes caked in mud,
her hair plastered to her skull,
where has she been,

and why has she come back?
She wanted to be left alone,
to make her own way,
her own mistakes,
and not always play

by somebody else's rules,
which, in any case, never made
much sense, to her mind,
though she went along with them,
until now, so as not

to create a stir. Blend in,
she told herself. Remain calm.
What she really wanted
was to disappear into the woodwork,
the way a grasshopper, sensing danger,

will disappear into the weeds,
or a bird, in a split second,
will dart into the trees.
The distance between here and there
is the distance between life and death.

I'm lost, she moans,
and will not listen to reason.
To argue with her
is to commit treason.

(September 29)

THE WORD

Be patient, I remind myself.
Patient. Give her a chance,
she's trying as hard as she can,
though the word she's looking for

stubbornly refuses to reveal itself,
digging ever deeper into its
hiding place, the way some fish
dig ever deeper into the dirt
at the bottom of the sea.

Sometimes, when all else fails,
we drive to the mall,
which used to annoy me
but now, through her eyes,
I see as a chance to get out,

meet people, and feel again
that life is good, no matter
what she believes or doesn't believe.
Life is more than she was
prepared to settle for,

more than television,
more than mystery novels,
more than long hours
lying in bed, or sitting
at the kitchen table, brooding.

If she doesn't speak her mind,
nobody will know what she thinks
or what she feels. To find
the word, let it go.

(October 6)

THE FOREST IN RUINS

I've found the card that she sent me
last Christmas, with a short note.
She was feeling much better, she said,
and hoped to be home in a few days.

A week at most. I wrote back,
though I knew it might not get there
in time. I told her about a dream
I'd had a couple of nights before,
in which she and I, along with ten others,

all from the same town, though strangers
to each other, were being led into a tropical
rain forest, where the foliage was so thick,
so lush, the sun had trouble getting through.
The trees had dark green, oval-shaped leaves

as big as elephant paws, and red flowers
of an intensity I had never seen before.
Parrots, perched high in the trees,
called to us in a language we could almost
understand. We let the others go ahead,

while we fell back, held by the beauty
all around us. At a fork in the road we turned
left instead of right, as the others had done.
We wanted to be alone. A few hundred yards
brought us to where a wall had been built,

made of old wooden beams, to block the way.
Yellow police tape warned us to stay out.
But as there was no one to stop us, we skirted
the wall, through the thorny underbrush,
we were so curious to see what was

on the other side, like children who,
blindfolded, try to guess what will be revealed.
What we found, though, was a forest in ruins,
the trees stripped of their leaves,
many limbs ripped off and scattered

everywhere, at odd angles to each other,
some standing almost straight up, impaled
in the earth by the force of the wind.
The animals had all fled or been killed.
Squirrel monkeys lay curled on the ground,

as if waiting to be born. Parrots
had been blown from their perches
and killed. Flies buzzed around the bodies.
There seemed to be no end to the devastation.
We turned and followed the path back,

the way we had come in. The sun beat down
very hard on our heads. The least spark, we knew,
could set everything on fire. It seemed we would never
get to the place where we had begun.

(October 13)

OVEREXTENDED

She sighs and straightens her back.
She's taken on too much, again.
For more than an hour now
she's been chopping, slicing, mixing,

measuring, sifting, and stirring,
focused on what needs to be done,
rather than what she can do with some
semblance of enjoyment. The contraption
for peeling and coring apples malfunctions,

digging too deep, cutting away too much
of the white, juicy flesh. The zucchini,
which had seemed so firm on the outside,
two mornings ago when she bought it,
is soft and mushy inside. The onion

keeps slipping from her grasp
as she chops. The gas makes her eyes
water and sting. What else can go wrong,
she asks herself, when she cuts her finger,
in a careless moment. But she is not ready

to call for help. Once she makes up her mind
there's very little that will get her to admit
defeat. She cleans the cut, stanches the wound,
and looks forward to sitting down at table,
when she'll be able to present the hoped-for dish

to her guest, see the look of gratitude in his eyes,
and feel she's done the best that she could,
which in the past, as she remembers it,
was all that anyone ever wanted.

(October 20)

BEFORE THE EARTH FROZE

Who can say when the tracks were made?
Some time before the earth froze, weeks,
months, or even years ago. The size
and depth of the impressions suggest

a heavy-set woman; not young.
The straight line of movement indicates
purpose; nothing haphazard. Until
almost the end, when the forest becomes
thicker and darker, and she loses

her way, and lurches from side to side.
Perhaps, in the dark, she feared the animals
that she had heard so much about,
the bears and the wolves,
the cougars and the snakes,

or perhaps she simply grew tired
and would have liked to lie down,
rest a moment, and listen
to the birds in the trees
and the rustling of the leaves.

Did I know her? I thought I did,
because I loved her. But love is never
enough. She was alone, in her mind,
and had no reason to hope
it might be otherwise.

She had played along, as true as anyone,
but the end, she knew, was near,
when the wind and the rain would come
and wash away all remembrance.

(October 27)

NO BEGINNING, NO END

She went inside, locking the door.
If I was who I said I was,
why had she never seen me before?
A walk around the block would do me good,

we both agreed. It was raining
but not hard. The wind had shifted
to the north, bringing colder, arctic air
that blew right through my poor hat.
The traffic was heavy on Champlain,

a steady stream that had no beginning
and no end. If I lost my balance,
as I clung to the edge of the sidewalk,
I might fall in front of a car and just like that,
as if by magic, all my troubles would be over.

Down Sainte Croix the traffic was light
to nonexistent. A woman I knew, a neighbor,
came toward me, her dog on a leash.
I asked his name, not for the first time.
We can be glad it's not snow, she said,

pulling her jacket tight around her shoulders.
In a shelter in a far corner of the parking lot
smokers congregated and made small talk.
Two or three stood outside the shelter,
in the rain, as if to punish themselves

for their bad behavior, or just because
it was too crowded inside. Farther down,
along the back road, a family of pheasants,
mama, papa, and six fledglings,
scurried to find a way down into the marsh.

I was cold, with the wind in my face,
but now, at least, I had something
I could tell her, something that might
please her and jog her memory.

(November 3)

WHITE NOISE

When she discovered that the white noise
not only did not
stop her from hearing the voices
but made her listen more closely,

in case they were talking about her,
saying things that were not true,
or at best half true,
with the aim of undermining her,
and sending her further into a tailspin,

she felt the wiser course of action
would be to accept her loss,
quietly, without protest, keeping
all her wits about her,
the way tulips will close up at night,

to retain whatever light and heat
they've captured during the day,
so that her enemies, who seemed
to be multiplying by the hour,
could do her no further harm.

She felt something funny in one ear,
a buzzing, a grinding the likes of which
she had never experienced before.
Was it a stroke? The flu? Chronic
fatigue? Or something else?

She stood up and announced to the others,
whom she had always thought of as friends,
but now believed otherwise, that she did not
feel well and wanted to go home.
Everyone stopped talking and looked at her.

She swayed back and forth, and we were
afraid she would fall. She took a step
toward the hallway, where she had hung
her coat, turned and looked at me.
I hurried to her side. I thought

we should go to the hospital,
but she said no, and she seemed
so sure of herself, so set,
I gave in and went along.

(November 10)

SLEEP, MY LOVE

I shake her knee
but she just stares back at me.
Don't go to sleep yet!
The show's hardly begun!

There was a time, not long ago,
when she was the star of the show,
the one who could take an idea,
and turn it into something grand,
the way a sunflower seed,

so small in the palm of the hand,
will keep growing until it is
as tall as a woman, or a man.
Whatever the obstacle, whatever
the hurdle, whatever the puzzle,

she persisted. She never gave in
or gave up. And what she did,
though often hard, she did with joy
in her heart. Everyone felt better
in her presence. She made people laugh.

She could have been black or white
or brown or yellow, male or female,
or something in between,
it would not have mattered,
for she was the spirit of adventure.

She sleeps a lot of the time now,
but I'm okay with that.
There's such a feeling of warmth
whenever I'm close to her.

(November 17)

ALLY

Because it is made of crystal,
not glass,
and because it was a gift
from her mother,

more than fifty years ago,
when she lived in a different town,
with a different husband,
facing different challenges,
she keeps it tucked away,

in the back of a drawer, in a box
with no name, hidden but not
forgotten. Whatever healing energy
it had to give, it's already given,
and now it's just a stone,

about the size of a thumbnail,
half an inch thick, oval in shape,
purple below, white above,
with raised dots over the uneven
surface, which sparkle like silver

in the light. The setting is silver,
in two rounds, the lower round
like beads strung together.
If I look closely enough,
I can see a moose

emerging from the purple haze,
with its antlers tilted into the white
above. Through all her troubles,
in the distant past, the not so distant
past, and the present, when the world

sometimes seemed to be collapsing
around her, she's taken the moose
as her symbol of strength
and endurance – her ally.

(November 24)

CLOUD OF FORGETTING

I kneel by the sofa where she lies,
one hand on her ankle,
the other on her knee.
She's quiet now, breathing

more easily, doing her best to forget
the angry words she shouted at me,
when it was not even me
she was angry with, but
someone else, an old friend,

who had gone off script,
thoughtlessly, and said things
that she found hurtful.
I could have intervened,
but I didn't see what was happening

until too late. Besides, it's not my part
to protect her every step of the way.
That would be asking too much.
If that seems heartless, I really
don't know what to say.

Let me pull the blanket up,
around her shoulders, and stay
a while longer, as she drifts away
on her cloud of forgetting.
Without forgetting, there is no

deliverance. But I am, I suppose,
the enemy of forgetting, someone
who, almost against his will, remembers
what she so desperately wants to forget.

(December 1)

FAT, WET FLAKES

The menace of a dark snow cloud
made her turn back from her walk,
and in her confusion she worried
that she might already be lost.

An hour ago, when she left the house,
the sky was clear, the wind calm,
the temperature barely below freezing.
She kept to the main trail, on the look-out
for the pond where the ducks swim

and the moose come to drink in the fall
before it freezes over. For too long
she'd been confined to the house,
unable to get out, until it had become
a sort of prison, though with a jailkeeper,

she had to admit, who was much kinder
and more attentive than she deserved.
All she wanted, she said, was to get
a breath of fresh air, and so one day,
while the jailkeeper was working

in the backyard, she put on her coat,
opened the door, and walked out.
I have to get moving, she told herself,
or I'll die of stasis, whatever that means.
In the house she didn't have much to do.

Read novels. Watch television. Sleep.
She had no energy to do anything creative,
or even cook. But the more she sat around,
or slept, the weaker she felt. Her legs
sometimes gave out, coming down

the stairs, and she had to hold on tight
to the railing to keep from falling.
A fall like that would be the end of her,
or the beginning of the end. No,
the end had already begun.

She wasn't dressed for bad weather,
she had left the house in such a hurry.
Now that it had turned nasty, however,
with the wind kicking up, and the snow
beginning to fall, fat, wet flakes of snow,

that smacked her in the face like
imitation confetti, she was sorry
she hadn't grabbed a pair of gloves
and some sort of hat on the way out.

                                                (December 8)

THE MENTAL LIFE
OF PLANTS AND WORMS

I couldn't stop yawning.
I wasn't bored, no, no,
that wasn't it. How could I
be bored, when every day

we had something new,
an appointment to keep,
a friend to meet,
a book to read,
a movie to watch.

I was a little tired, I'll admit,
but not unusually so.
I'd had a good night's sleep,
and woke to a vivid dream,
in which I was in my old

bookstore, talking to a customer,
deploring the sad state of affairs,
the paucity of quality paperbacks,
when in walked a young writer,
in town for a festival of authors,

searching for a book by somebody
called Stuart A. Guest, whom I'd frankly
never heard of before. Or maybe
it was Stuart N. Guest, he wasn't sure.
I was very sorry, I said, at which point

the promising young writer
disappeared behind a stack of books,
then reappeared, just as suddenly,
with a copy of the book by the author
he was looking for, the title of which,

once I'd registered it, I promptly
forgot. I couldn't stop yawning.
Maybe I'd had too much to eat,
but no, that wasn't it. I'd had
a plate of linguini, with a meat

and tomato sauce, topped with
grated cheddar cheese. A modest
helping, nothing extravagant.
A glass of red wine. Frozen yogurt
for dessert, with raspberries. Maybe

I wasn't getting enough oxygen,
it was so cold out and the wind blew
through the cracks around the windows
and the doors and the furnace ran
almost non-stop, pumping out

hot, dry air. Or maybe the book
she was reading to me, which I
had welcomed at first, was about
a topic I had little interest in, namely,
the mental life of plants and worms.

I thought this was stretching it a bit,
though that just shows you what I know.
Apparently, worms have a central
organizing cluster of nerve cells that functions
very much like a brain, and underlies a certain

primitive form of intelligence. Well,
maybe it's true. I couldn't stop yawning.
Annoyed, she said, why don't you
go to bed, we'll talk about it tomorrow.

(December 15)

THE DAYS GROW LONGER

Everyone leaves me, I am always
alone. Strange, isn't it, the way
deaths occur in clusters.
A cat can tell when we're not

feeling well. The days grow
longer, but mine grow shorter.
I want somebody to say something
to me, tell me what he thinks.
It is the tone of voice that matters,

not the meaning of the words.
This is the worst time of the year,
I have so many letters to write,
so many gifts to give. I feel
like a prisoner in my own house.

The sad thing about not being able
to drive is that I'm stuck where I am,
with nowhere to go. The word *should*
should be eliminated from my vocabulary.
My feet are cold, but no matter what I do

they still feel cold. For the first time
in my life I would like to go south
for the winter. Trees know
when one of their kind is sick,
don't ask me how. Sometimes

the tallest, strongest-looking tree
is the one that falls. The appearance
of strength masks an inner weakness,
a dry rot, so that even a gentle wind
might be enough to knock it over.

Whatever happens, happens,
whether I am the root cause or not.
When I turn off the television,
the silence is deafening.

(December 22)

REAL LIFE

I will have to abandon my dream,
if I want to go on living. Real life,
compared to the dream, is dull,
monotonous, hardly worth the effort.

The dream seems to be illuminated
from within, the way the warm, translucent
waters of the Caribbean, when calm, are lit
from below, revealing wondrous forms
too rich and varied to be believed.

What is the dream? It is always
the same and always different.
I am in another city, another country,
where people recognize me
for who I am, and value me,

where people do not hesitate
to speak to me, openly, where people
love me and look after me when I'm
in need. All my wishes, whether modest
or not so modest, are fulfilled,

as they never are, in real life.
It's too good to be true, but it is true,
in the dream, which stays with me
all day, like a drug. I never want
to let it go, but I must. Must open

my eyes, look, and see, all around me,
a world of small, everyday things,
each as remarkable as a bird
perched on the arm of a man.

(December 29)

WHAT I WANTED TO SAY

I tried to talk with her last night,
and then again this morning.
My words were weak, ineffectual,
like someone calling out a warning

after the storm has already past.
She knew more about the dangers
than I, but had reached a point
where she simply did not care.
I've had a good life, she'd say,

when pressed. I have no regrets.
I'm not afraid, don't worry. She
liked to watch murder mysteries
because the format guaranteed
that the culprit would be found.

The fun was in trying to guess
who it was. None of the violence
was real. What I wanted to say
was simple enough. It's essential
to keep moving, if only around

the house, from room to room.
Take another look at the art work
on the walls, or the tiny bottles
on the glass ledge in the window.
Step outside onto the back deck,

and watch the moon in the trees
as it rises for the night. Sometimes
bats swoop low, so quietly,
so darkly, you can barely see them.

(January 5)

THESE VARIOUS PROOFS

She is at least grudgingly aware
that many of the things she used to do,
by herself, she can no longer do.
To get in the car and go visit

a friend, on the spur of the moment,
is a dream she abandoned years ago.
The ice on the path to the studio
makes getting there impossible,
and even when it is bare,

as with this early January thaw, she's afraid
to go out, because she might lose her balance
and fall. From experience she knows well
that she might take a sudden dizzy spell,
and need a helping hand,

which would rankle. Sometimes, for lunch,
she feels inspired to concoct a more complicated,
hearty soup, one better suited for chilly winter
weather, but before she can finish, with
so much cutting and slicing,

more often than not she runs out of steam and
gives up, in tears. It's for me to finish the job,
or not. Later, after our rest, we like to get out,
into the fresh air, and if it is a nice day,
walk around the block,

or down the street to where there is
a path along the river, which is always
a wonder to behold, at this time of year,
with its massive ice flows, which are like
the thoughts and images

that float through our unconscious, night
after night, when we are not paying attention.
But we get down to the river less often
these days, and then only with a walker,
which at first seemed to be

an admission of some sort of defeat, but now
seems perfectly okay. Simple, everyday
tasks, such as opening the milk carton,
with its stubborn pull-tab, she finds
difficult, even exasperating,

because of the weakness in her fingers,
and her wrist. And yet, faced with these
various proofs of decline, and others
as telling, she feels no different,
she claims, than she felt

fifty years ago, or sixty, when she came
into her prime. Life has been good to her,
despite the losses, the aches, and the pains,
and she wouldn't change a thing.

(January 12)

I CAN'T SAY I'M SORRY

I was riding in the first car,
alone in the back seat. The driver
was a stranger but I trusted him
to take me where I wanted to go.

I told him to turn left at the light
and continue along Mountain Road.
My daughter and her husband
followed in the car behind,
then my son and his wife,

then all the others. Set back from
the road, hidden among trees, the old
home for orphans and foundlings,
an impressive building in its day,
four stories high, with a large turret

at one corner, stood abandoned,
sheets of plywood over the windows,
a sad and ugly sight. A few blocks
further along I told the driver to stop
and I went into the health food store.

I searched the shelves and the bins
but could not find what I was looking for.
At the corner of Mountain Road and Reade,
behind the funeral home, in a sudden rain,
the parking lot was full. Cars lined

both sides of the street. I tried to think
who might have died recently. The old
strip club, which had had such a loyal
clientele over the years, was finally closed,
and I can't say I'm sorry. A bulldozer

kept up its steady work of destruction,
tearing the building apart, piece by
piece, until it was nothing but
a pile of rubble and a cloud of dust.
Just beyond the highway overpass,

in a shabby-looking mini-mall,
the part of the building that had once
been home to the town's only half-decent
bookstore was vacant. Now what
were we supposed to do, other than

complain? On top of the mountain
we stopped for one last look at the city
below, so spread out, and I felt the loss
of all the people and places I had loved.

(January 19)

A FIGHTING CHANCE

My whistle failed to elicit a response.
I tried again. A chickadee answered
from inside the forsythia bush.
A dozen pigeons, neatly lined up

on the top bar of the swing set,
stared at me in a calculated display
of indifference. They knew what
I was up to, and what they needed
to do, to get what they wanted.

On top of the house next door
another dozen waited, expectantly.
It was a thin whistle, which left them
guessing as to my wishes. Was I trying
to welcome them, or scare them off?

I re-shaped my mouth and tried again.
High in the spruce tree crows cawed
impatiently, angrily. From the window
of the upstairs bedroom my wife watched.
A blue jay, on a chair in the neighbor's

backyard, made a sound like a yodel,
melodious and seductive, before reverting
to the more familiar shrill cry, like a rusty
clothesline. A male pheasant, with its white
ring around the neck, hid in plain sight

behind the japonica bush, sure
of its camouflage. If I moved slowly,
I hoped the bird would not fly away
in a thundering fright. I wanted
the pheasant, along with any starlings

and chickadees that might be nearby,
to have a fighting chance at the feed
(black sunflower seeds, wild bird mix,
peanuts in the shell, leftover crusts
of bread broken into bite-sized pieces)

when I cast it, by the handful, across
the white plastic table by the back fence
and onto the ground, before the pigeons
descended *en masse*. Although, as my
wife had often reminded me, pigeons

need to eat too, like all the other birds,
if we do not want them to die. The cold
weather, in and of itself, will kill off
more than a few. Don't be so stingy.

(January 26)

THE ART OF CAMOUFLAGE

I will change names, places, dates,
I will change tenses, persons, voices,
I will change genders,
I will change days of the week,

I will change months of the year,
I will change seasons if need be.
I will conceal my sources,
I will become an expert
in the art of camouflage.

No one but myself will know
the words I have been given,
in the beginning, to look at,
to interrogate, and to find
the story they hide,

which is there for me and me alone,
the story I want to tell, about her,
about us, about our life together,
about how we look after each other.
Although it starts with someone else,

the story will be my own.
I will tell it the way I see it
and the way I feel it. No one
has heard it before, or suspected
that it could be so. I will say

what I have to say, even if I expose
myself, or her, like the pheasant
behind the japonica bush, hiding among
bare branches, in plain sight, visible to all.

(February 2)

ODE TO ICE

The man thinks of stepping on the ice.
He thinks of falling.
The woman thinks of calling a friend.
She thinks of the burden she will carry.

Ice covers the ground but does not
protect what's already in the ground,
the way a snowfall protects.
Ice makes venturing forth less
tempting; breeds stasis.

Under the ice the earth turns
in on itself. Things look dead,
but somehow, for the most part,
live on. Birds die when
they don't get enough to eat.

Plants die when they are left
unprotected and unloved. Hold
my arm; if one falls, both fall.
The distance from the house to the car
seems as far as the nearest star.

The promise of spring, slowly
awakening, is an invitation
to dream. The days grow longer,
the sun shines more brightly,
the ice melts. The future, she thinks,

begins any time now. It's always
possible, he thinks, notwithstanding
appearances. The cracks in the tips
of his fingers start to heal.

(February 9)

THE LAST THING SHE WANTS

She doesn't growl at me any more than usual.
Hardly at all.
A gentle – or not so gentle – reminder
that it has been how many days now

since I last did the laundry.
The basket's full
and smells when she opens it.
She has nothing to wear, not even
a bra, on the off chance that she might

want to go out. There's dirt everywhere,
dust balls on the stairs,
cat hairs floating in the rays of the sun,
and she has trouble breathing.
When was the last time I vacuumed?

She can't remember, nor can I.
A week, at least.
And why do I cook the same thing
night after night when I know
she has no appetite. If only

she would tell me what she likes.
But no,
it's either too dry or too oily, seldom
the right mix. Maybe, she thinks,
we should call Meals on Wheels.

Give ourselves a break. She appreciates
everything I do,
but it's too much for one person,
as witness the house crumbling,
and the last thing she wants,

she says, is to live (or die) in squalor.
I can deny
the obvious, if I want, that's my
business. Life is what happens when
we look the other way, or something

like that. In the kitchen window, under
the spruce tree,
six female pheasants are digging
and digging for yesterday's seeds.

(February 16)

ODE TO HANDS

With hands like this she could be an artist.
The thumb small,
with wrinkled knuckle and cracked nail.
The fingers long, thick, hairless.

The skin on the back of the hand
translucent,
crisscrossed with fine lines,
old scars, and dark squiggles of blood
as they go down to do their work.

These hands have an energy,
a vitality,
that flows into them and through them
to whatever they touch, a piece of clay
to be shaped, a canvas to be painted,

a print to be pressed, or someone
to be loved.
Small hands are made for reaching
into the cookie jar. Big hands
are for chopping wood, painting houses,

milking cows, shooting basketballs,
and the like.
A helping hand is what anyone
would hope for, in times of trouble.
The thought of her, beaten down

by life, makes my hand tremble.
A drowning man,
to save himself, might reach his hand
towards an imagined rescue,
before going down for good.

In the painting the man lays his hand,
ever so lightly,
on the breast of his wife,
while she rests her hand on his.

(February 23)

PERHAPS

She could easily have fallen on the steps
coming out of Artemis's house.
She could be on the way to the hospital
this very moment. Somebody, eventually,

will think of contacting me.
She's never been this late before.
She was supposed to call me at four
and let me know when
to pick her up. Something

must have happened and I can only
imagine the worst. Perhaps she had a heart attack
and she's lying on the floor in the living room
and the ambulance is on the way
and nobody knows if she'll live or die.

Perhaps she hitched a ride with Lucy
and they were talking and Lucy
ran a red light and hit a brand-new
Lexus GX or a Land Rover
and threw her against the windshield

because she wasn't wearing a seatbelt,
which would not have been like her,
although recently, it's true, she's been very
forgetful. Perhaps fatigue
overtook her and she stretched out

on the bed in Artemis's spare
bedroom, in the basement, and fell asleep.
I pace back and forth in the hallway,
glancing out the window every so often.
I sit at a table in the sun porch

and wait. Perhaps something she ate
disagreed with her and she vomited
on the black pleated skirt
we had washed just yesterday.
It's five o'clock and she still hasn't called,

I don't know what to do with myself.
I'm too on edge to read or watch TV.
I should call Artemis
but just then a car pulls into the driveway
and Lucy gets out and helps my wife

out of the car, onto the sidewalk. "We talked
a long time," she smiles, as she brushes
past me, takes hold of the railing,
and climbs the stairs into the house.
Lucy grabs three old beat-up picture frames

from the back seat and wants to give them
to me. Perhaps we can find a use for them.
If we had a fireplace, I think,
I'm sure we would have no trouble.

(March 2)

HER SMILE

When the talk turns to sex and politics,
when the jokes become crude,
when she gets tired and her thoughts
begin to shoot off in all directions,

when the children who've been sitting
so quietly beside her on the bench
suddenly get up and run into the next room,
when she doesn't hear or understand
what someone has said,

she smiles her beautiful smile
and they think she knows more
than she lets on. They think
she possesses the wisdom
that comes with age.

Who can resist her smile?
The way the lip curls in and back,
revealing the small, even teeth,
which she has cared for, faithfully,
all the years of her life. Friends

and strangers want to photograph her,
just to capture her perfect smile.
There's nothing fake about her smile,
nothing put on. Her smile is never
at someone's expense, to hurt.

Her smile means she's happy
to be where she is, with the people
she's with, even if sometimes
she doesn't understand them,
and they don't understand her.

Her smile opens the way for her
into almost any room where people
have gathered. Everyone loves her smile,
because it is free of all pretense.

(March 9)

CHANCE STARS

To get them set up the way she wants
takes forever.
The gaps in her thinking are like
the gaps in clouds, through which

chance stars appear briefly, and are gone.
It's no use
trying to get them back. Might as well
try to stop the earth from rotating.
Some last longer than others,

for example, her father, who stands out
most brightly,
with his happy smile, sitting in a lawn chair
at the cabin by the lake, dressed in
high leather boots, white trousers,

a black cardigan, and an old fedora,
with his fishing license
stuck to the hat band. But she forgets
the names of my father and my mother,
shown together on the middle shelf,

in the early days of their marriage,
dressed shabbily,
but happy looking, in love.
She takes down the photo of my son
and myself on the streets of Philadelphia,

the year he graduated from Wharton,
gives it a dusting,
and puts it back. She does the same
with the photo of my daughter,
taken at the time of her graduation

from high school, before she went away
to university
and disappeared from my life.
She remembers her name but not
where the photo was taken.

On the bottom shelf, to the right of center,
her own daughter
sits in a folding chair, some forty years ago,
with her husband in a chair next to her,
and their two children, one sitting, one standing,

in sturdy galvanized-zinc tubs,
and behind them
a picket fence painted brown, and
thick maple trees providing ample shade.

(March 16)

A MISTAKE

The whole thing's a mistake,
a trick.
If only she had died that time
in hospital, when she was sick,

she wanted to, she had seen
what it was like,
she was ready, a little nudge
was all she would need,
she said, to tip her over the edge.

When it didn't happen, as desired,
she wept.
It took courage to go on, not to die.
Life, lived well, might promise
some sort of wisdom, some vision,

but she isn't holding her breath.
A gray mist,
as thick as any on the high seas,
obscures the path she has chosen.
Her mind, once vibrant, has become

less reliable. Her body, once active,
has begun to break down.
So many things she'd been able to do
she can no longer do. Worst of all
is the feeling of isolation.

She will have to wait it out,
get used to it,
and remember she is not in command,
but something wholly other.

(March 23)

DON'T EVEN ASK

This could mean two things.
A friend might have called
and invited her out for a cup of coffee,
and she said yes, because she's been feeling

isolated and depressed. Or she might have had
another angina attack,
more severe that usual, and called an ambulance.
I was only gone an hour, running a few errands,
because we were out of some essentials,

such as milk, bread, butter, eggs, bird feed,
and some kind of protein.
The cat was waiting for me when I opened the door
and gave me an openly defiant look, as if to say,
I don't know where she went, don't even ask.

I looked upstairs, in both bedrooms, searched
the basement,
in case she might have fallen down the stairs,
but it was obvious the house was empty.
It felt empty. All the energy was drained out of it,

like an empty, upside-down water bottle.
I would have thought
that she would leave a note, or something,
telling me where she was, if she was going to go
away like that. But I suppose, if it was an emergency,

she might not have had time. So here I am,
not sure what to do.
Maybe she's in the studio, but that's not likely,
with the path still covered in ice and a dusting of snow.
She hasn't been to the studio for weeks, for months,

so why today of all days would she decide to wander
out back?
It's not as if she's run out of ideas, and can't think
what she wants to do next. She just doesn't have
the strength she used to have. For a long time

she worked in oil pastels but now she "inhabits boxes,"
as she describes it.
I liked the oil pastels, because of the way she could create
such deep, rich colors and such interesting textures.
The trouble is that oil pastels, like spray paints (another
of her favorites)

can be hazardous to the health, so I don't blame her.
It's true no doubt
that her confusion stems in part from inhaling noxious
chemicals. If she's not in the studio, I'll call the hospital.

(March 30)

STRANGERS IN THE NIGHT

It's not the first time she's told me
the story of her life,
and I'm sure it won't be the last.
"You don't have to listen to this,"

she says, not sure whether or not
I've heard it before.
After twenty-five years together,
we still feel, at times, like strangers
who have just met at some

concert or film and are trying,
awkwardly,
to get to know each other. I take
whatever I want from her story,
whatever strikes me, and I feel less

distant from her, though I know there are
vast areas
where neither one of us wants to go.
We are passengers on a bus, travelling
to a place we've never been, excited,

in a heightened state of awareness,
but at the same time
wary of what awaits us, unsure
if we will be able to tell the difference
between what is real and what is not real.

She had a full, rich life before we met,
most of which
I know nothing about and never will.
So who is she? My wife, but that's just
a fact. Inside her head, where she lives,

who is she? It's not her intention,
I'm sure,
to shut me out, but every day
she remembers less and less.

(April 6)

ODE TO CATS

The woman steps onto the back deck
with a flashlight,
searches the ground below the picket fence
but finds nothing out of the ordinary.

In her dream there were three cats,
including her own Ginger,
sitting close together under the fence,
transfixed by something happening
just on the other side, some animal,

some commotion that was both intriguing
and frightening.
In the beam of the flashlight she could see
what it was, a snake almost hidden
in a pile of leaves, only the large head

plainly visible. She told herself
stay calm,
there are no poisonous snakes
where we live, but for the cats
the danger, or the fear, had more

to do with being swallowed alive,
or strangled.
First Ginger, then the others jumped
onto the deck, seeking protection.
Should she let them into the house,

until the danger had passed?
The tri-color cat
seemed ready to stand her ground,
but the little white cat, a kitten,
trembled in fear. Animals are no different

from humans in their ability to feel
pain and pleasure,
misery and happiness, fear and its opposite,
though humans have the ability to name
what they feel, and to stew over it.

Some cats are young, some cats are old,
some cats are tame,
some cats are wild, some cats are friendly
and some are not. Every unfriendly cat
has a story to tell, of what makes him

the way he is, or she. Friendly cats too
have a history,
which would include, almost without
exception, being well loved.

(April 13)

IT'S ALL RIGHT

A cry rises from the bedroom at the top of the stairs,
then a thud.
The house seems to shudder, then become
settled again, the way a ship, when it hits a rock

underwater, or a long-forgotten sunken treasure,
or debris
from a previous shipwreck, will wobble
a moment, before regaining its balance
and moving on. It may be damaged, but not

fatally, it's hoped. More than likely it's nothing
to worry about,
and there's no need to tell anybody, no need
to broadcast the news, which would only cause
unnecessary panic, adding to the loss of life,

when the ship finally does sink, as it must,
in time.
Think of all the passengers, in the ship's hold,
asleep, unaware of the unfolding catastrophe.
Why wake them with cries for help,

when there's nothing they can do,
in the end,
but watch as fate works its way out?
A trip to emergency might be in order,
and then again it might not be.

Once the house shakes and shudders, even though
it steadies again,
it will never be the same. Something has happened
and the beams and the walls will not forget.
She may die in her sleep, or while meditating,

or while taking a shower, or coming down the stairs.
She may faint
or have a stroke, she may die tomorrow,
but it's all right, she says, she's ready.

(April 20)

SHE CONTINUES

In spite of these many obstacles,
such as poor memory,
failing eyesight, shortness of breath,
chronic weakness in the legs, dizziness

brought on by a diuretic given to counter
the shortness of breath,
bowels that are sometimes overactive,
sometimes locked in place for days
on end, with no relief in sight,

in spite of all this, she continues,
every morning,
to get up, write in her journal,
meditate, stretch, jot down
her agenda for the day, get dressed,

make her way, slowly, down the stairs,
holding tight
to the railing and the newly installed
"grip" - in case her head swims
and her body wants to fall.

She continues to find reasons
to go on living,
foremost being concern for her family
and what sort of legacy she might leave
if she were to do away with herself.

She continues to want to get out
and do things,
meet a friend for a cup of coffee,
go to a movie, take in a play,
drive somewhere to watch the sunset.

She continues to enjoy the outdoors,
sitting on the back deck,
watching the tulips come up,
the allium, and the scilla. She continues.

(April 27)

ODE TO BODIES

Bodies caught in a glacier after a fall,
or buried
under tons of snow in an avalanche,
or drowned in a northern lake

after a boating mishap, or locked
in a freezer
to hide the evidence of a crime,
keep the look of life-in-death
for years, with rosy cheeks,

clear skin, and bright eyes, until
one day
the glacier shifts, the snow
melts, the lake runs dry,
and someone opens the freezer

and what chance has concealed,
or evil intent,
is revealed. Bodies felled
in an instant, by a heart attack,
or by a blow to the head,

taken by surprise, remain
intact,
their faces showing, perhaps,
a puzzlement, or a growing sense
of something large, pressing down on them.

Bodies that die peaceful deaths,
free of pain,
asleep in their beds, surrounded,
if only in a dream, by those they love,
are most to be envied. Bodies

that have been tampered with,
mutilated,
tortured, shot, or in any way
disrespected, making fear
or dread the last emotion

they will ever feel, are most
to be pitied.
There is nothing to be said of them,
other than to lament their fate.

(May 4)

STANDING HERE AT THE CUTTING BOARD

I picked up the knife she had dropped,
a long knife,
a quite ordinary kitchen knife but sharp,
good for slicing bread, carving roasts,

cutting cucumbers, and chopping onions,
an all-purpose knife,
but heavy, especially in hands that were
shaky to begin with. Sharper than
the steak knives that too often

did not slice or cut at all but tore,
they were so dull.
There were tears in her eyes and not just
from the onions. A cut like the one
she'd given herself doesn't hurt at first,

but in a while begins to throb
and to ache,
and the blood keeps coming,
from under the too-thin, too-narrow
bandage, which is not sufficient.

Why do I go on living, she wanted to know,
looking at me.
Here I am, standing here at the cutting board,
like a dummy, with not enough strength
to open a jar of pickles. Why do I bother,

I don't even like pickles. Slicing off
the tip of my finger
was not an accident, but a wish to draw
blood, to feel something, anything,
after days and weeks of feeling nothing,

unable to climb out of the hole I'm in,
the pit.
You try your best, I know,
but sometimes it is not enough.

(May 11)

WHAT ONCE WAS

She is far too sociable
a woman
not to chafe at the limits
her condition imposes on her.

What she wants is to get out
more often,
see friends, talk and laugh,
forget her troubles. Gossip
a little, tell stories. Inside,

everything is always the same,
so ho-hum,
nothing much to stir the emotions
except the occasional phone call
connecting her to the outside world,

reminding her she is still alive,
still here.
With the coming of spring, she likes
to walk to the bottom of the street
and on warm days along the path

by the river, where the tide rises
and falls,
rises and falls, twice a day,
the way her spirit, the longing
in her to be part of things,

rises and falls, rises and falls,
like clockwork,
where fireflies used to light up
the marshland, rich in sea water,
and where birds used to make

their nests, before the road
ruined it all,
scattering hapless creatures to the wind,
a sad reminder of what once was.

(May 18)

ODE TO LAUGHTER

Comical interlude, she said.
Laugh now,
while there's still something left
to laugh about. We used to think

that things could not get
much worse,
but now we know better.
We can laugh or weep,
but laughter is more cathartic.

Laughter does not deny reality,
like fantasy,
but makes it into something
more human, and therefore
more tolerable, like clean water.

Laughter points to one conclusion:
whatever is is,
the past is nothing like what
it used to be, and the future
is anyone's guess.

Laughter lurks in alleyways
scrounging
its next meal, in dark corners,
in dumpsters that promise surprise
after surprise, like poetry.

Laughter lasts longer than lies,
which age badly,
like wine from an inferior grape.
Laughter tells the truth, madly.

(May 25)

ODE TO NEIGHBORS

She walks to the bottom of the street,
scans
the neighboring yards, front and back,
looks to see if there is not someone

she could call to, engage in small
talk,
and speak her mind. For too long
she's been confined to the house,
with nothing much to do,

other than watch television, read,
sleep,
and maybe, on occasion, make supper.
It's hard to muster the energy
to get out of the house,

in her condition, but once she sets
foot
on the street, there's a lightness to her step
that she seldom experiences
when she's cooped up in the house.

The street, however, has gone through many changes
in recent months, and several of the people
she was once close to are no longer
with us. Eric, next door, lost his house

when he stopped paying his bills, now it stands empty,
largely neglected by the new, absentee
owner. Lucille, our neighbor to the south, toward
the river, has moved to an old people's home,

which was not unexpected, at her age. The property now belongs
to her son, who rents to his son and daughter-in-law,
whom we hardly ever see. Roger and Roberta,
in the next house down, enjoy a lively conversation,

whenever it happens, and if Elaine is lucky, she will find them
at the door, though these days they spend
most of their time on the back deck,
in a screened-in area, free of mosquitoes.

Paul, across the street, always has a friendly word,
in the midst of his worries about his wife,
who has fallen ill. Lucy, who used to live
next to Paul, one house up from the river,

sold everything and moved into an apartment, tired
from years of taking care of the property on her own,
though she's still fit as a fiddle and able to handle
anything she sets her mind to. John and Maggie,

in the brick house across from us, are the best
neighbors
we could ask for, they keep an eye on us,
if we're in trouble, they are ready to help
when we call on them and even when

we don't. I mustn't forget our closest,
and dearest,
neighbor, another Roger, who lives underground,
in Lucille's basement, like a gnome, guarding his
secret for equanimity, and who only comes out

when least expected. Though fewer than before,
the neighbors
that remain, the ones we know, make us
want to stay here, in our little big house.

(June 1)

THE BUMBLEBEE

I see a bumblebee
flying
around the house,
from room to room,

from flower to flower,
searching
for something it cannot find,
some way out, or failing that,
some food, some pollen,

to survive, until a door
opens,
or a window, for escape.
The flowers we've gathered,
a different sort for each room,

do not give the bee what it wants,
wilting,
fading, losing their petals,
losing even the sweet smell
they promised of spring.

The tulips in the kitchen,
fresh
from the garden, already
show some roughness around
the edges. The lilacs in the sun porch,

cut yesterday, have lost their luster,
overnight.
The carnations in the living room,
on the coffee table, are more black
than red, and should be tossed.

The chrysanthemums in the dining room,
set
in the middle of the round table,
look to be holding their own,
a brilliant yellow-gold color,

with dark green leaves interspersed.
Buzzing
around the mums, and over them,
the unhappy bee does not seem to think
there's anything worth stopping for.

More and more slowly it flies,
running
itself down. If I cannot capture it,
it will settle somewhere and die.

(June 8)

EVERYWHERE HE GOES

She's on the steps behind us,
smiling,
with her eyes shut tight
because of the late-afternoon sun.

It's a genuinely happy
smile,
on the occasion of my son's
visit, his second already
this year. He's seen enough

to realize it's not possible for us
to visit him,
so he visits us, as often as he can,
as he passes through our town,
on his way to his cabin in the woods,

where he likes to let his dog,
Sarge,
run free. Everywhere he goes
Sarge goes with him, in the car,
on the airplane, to the office. He's

so attached to him, he follows him
up the stairs
to the bathroom. In the picture we are
relaxed, standing at the curb, posing
for the camera, all smiles, with Sarge

sitting at attention. I'm so glad
my son
is doing well, and visits more often,
and we get a chance to know him better.

(June 15)

LOW TIDE

The tide is out by the time we get there.
Rocks
line the riverbed, along both sides.
The banks of mud are almost vertical,

where the water has washed away
all resistance,
in its rush to the sea, and only the grass,
on top of the mud, holds firm. In the middle,
where there is still some standing water,

it is no deeper than two or three feet.
Leviathan,
sea monster, lies with its belly cut open,
the same way a snake, a python,
must be cut open when it swallows

a human being whole, and becomes
so heavy,
so tied down, it cannot save itself
from a slow death. Cut open, turned
inside out, the belly of the river

displays the intestines, sculpted
by the sea
as it sucks the water to itself,
leaving an emptiness, as the heart
feels empty when hope slips away,

betrayed by gravity. The seagulls,
the herons,
the eagles too, what is there for them
to do, but wait for the tide to turn.

(June 22)

IT'S LATER THAN YOU THINK

Her friend, eyes narrowed and lip curled,
says nothing
but she doesn't have to. Everyone knows
what she thinks. It would be foolish

to put more money into repairs
and improvements
when it's possible, even likely
that the person who ends up buying
this old house, built as it is on such

a shaky foundation, will want to
tear it down
and build something more sturdy,
more modern in its place, for example,
a three story clapboard, with six condos

and a dental clinic to service an aging
population.
Time moves on, she's quick to add,
ticking our lives away day after day.
People grow anxious, and they want

something new, even if it is the
same old thing,
as monotonous as prairie grass.
It's all in the name of progress,
she laughs. Progress means you look

beyond the here and now, towards
the invisible future,
where things will be bigger and better.
It means you are never content
with the way things are, but always

want the latest, the shiniest. And even if
that future
proves to be illusory, you will still have
the satisfaction knowing you played the game.

(June 29)

HOT AND HUMID

She washes out her shirt and hangs it up
to dry,
using a clothespin to fasten the hanger
to the clothesline. With the hot sun

and steady wind it should be dry in an hour,
she hopes,
in time to wear to our friend's house for supper.
All day she's been fighting the hot and humid
weather, and fighting me because I do not

want to run the air conditioner non-stop,
worried
we might overload the electrical circuit and risk
a fire. If you're trying to kill me, you're doing
a good job of it, she cries, to which I have

no reply, other than get the air conditioner
set up in the window,
ready to start again. She lies on the bed,
with the fan turned on high, which, as she
rightly complains, does little more than move

the hot air around. She sleeps an hour or so,
then gets up,
wobbly, unsteady on her feet, and tries
one shirt after another, until she finds one
she likes, washes it and hangs it out to dry.

While she showers I get the air conditioner
going again,
though I'm still convinced my worries
about the wiring are well-founded,
for it's a circuit that includes, in one room,

the air conditioner, the clock radio, the fan,
and the overhead light,
and in a second room the computer, the phone,
and the overhead light. If one of these outlets
or switches dies, they will all die.

There is some comfort knowing we have
a smoke detector,
two fire extinguishers, two easy routes of escape,
front and back, and if we have to, we could
climb out the bedroom window onto

the roof of what we call the mud room
and wait
to be rescued, though perhaps at our age
that's not a very practicable alternative.

(July 6)

SHE'S BUSY NOW

She's busy now trying to remember
the names
that go with the photographs
she'd like to copy and send.

She remembers the faces, and what
she wants to say, but not
the names. She keeps drawing a blank.
Try as hard as she might,
she can not remember the names.

This photo, yes, this one, she used to know
very well.
The name starts with an "F." Maybe
Frances, or Francine, but no, neither
sounds right. She blames it on herself.

On her faulty memory. Everyone she
once knew
she's busy now forgetting. At times
she's able to catch a glimpse, a hint,
a fragment that flees from her

the moment she turns to look at it.
So many of her friends
are dying, one after the other, from one
illness or another – cancer, heart disease,
diabetes, kidney failure, depression,

you name it. Sometimes she shuffles
the photos
and the face that comes out on top
she's not looked at or thought about
in years. But the name remains hidden

in some dark corner of her brain,
complete,
indestructible, but beyond her reach,
like the ripest apple on the tree.

(July 13)

THEN LET IT GO

Now that she's found a solution to all
her problems
she feels she can begin to live again.
Everything that was dull, monotonous,

not worth the effort, now has
new life,
new sparkle, new promise, enough
to make her want to get up
out of her chair, look around, and ask

what is there to do now, in the short
time
I have left. Birds die before they know it,
but they go on singing, with no
hint of the fate that awaits them.

Even the crow cawing is not complaining,
but seeking
refuge in companionship. Roses burst from
the rosebush like exploding galaxies,
then die away, in the knowledge

they will come again, when the time
is ripe.
Dogs bark to let her know they are still
here, needing food and comforting.
Everything reminds her of earth's

bounty, and if at times she thinks about
death
it is with her newly won sense of equanimity.
Death is not a battle, not a massacre,
but joining with the rhythms of nature.

This life is the only one we know and
the only one
we need to know. It is precious,
tend to it, then let it go, like the roses.
Actions she once thought closed to her

she now finds possible. For example,
she might call
a friend, one she has not seen in months,
arrange to meet for coffee and talk as of old.

(July 20)

WEEDS, AND MORE WEEDS

Everything is dry. The garden
struggles
to stay alive, even with constant
watering. The grass has stopped

growing, for now, and to the west
wildfires
have forced many people from their homes.
Rain sometimes falls on us, but briefly,
almost nothing since the beginning of the month.

The sudden, intense downpours feel like
the almighty's
none-too-subtle jest. The earth
forms a crust which keeps the water
from penetrating to the roots of the plants.

The herbs, as they mature, turn brown, wilt
and fade. The sunflowers are smaller
than expected. The tomatoes are about
the size of walnuts. Weeds prove hardier,

and more plentiful – sorrel, pennywort, mullein,
hedge mustard, stinging nettle, tansy,
bladderwort, goldenrod, and feathery
horsetail, among others. The bird baths

have to be scrubbed and re-filled
every second day,
the birds use them so frequently in this heat.
Hornets and wasps drink from the water.

(July 27)

TOO BAD FOR THEM

She stands at the entrance to the basement
and wonders
if I know what it is that she wants
down below, in the cold and the dark.

Potatoes, I suggest. Carrots. Tomatoes.
Kidney beans.
A bottle of wine. Mosquito repellent.
Paint. Vise grips. The hammer. Nothing
clicks. It seemed very important,

a moment ago, she says, but now I can't
remember.
There's something wrong with my brain.
All my friends have forgotten me,
she says. They have such busy,

interesting lives, and here I sit,
going to pieces.
If they don't want to call me,
too bad for them. I may be slow,
I may be dull, but they'd be surprised

what I know, if they would give me
half a chance.
To hell with them. Something saps
her energy, drags her down, weakens
her will to live. Every catastrophe

has an upside, something that lifts
her spirits.
First, there's the rain, then the rainbow.
Not every time, but often enough.

(August 3)

ODE TO HIDING PLACES

He's always looking for a way
to steal
a few moments for himself. Day
and night he listens and watches, to see

whether or not there's any sign of a crisis,
any turn
for the worse that should be dealt with urgently,
while at the same time doing what he can
to keep up with the chores around the house

as they arise. Sometimes the demands
outpace his capacity,
and he knows he has to find a place
where he can be alone, where he can
make sense of things and try not to be

swept along like a log in a swift-moving
flooded river
clogged with mud, dead fish, and animal
carcasses. He might shut himself in his room,
and work on his novel which he and only he

has any idea even exists. Or he might step onto
the back deck,
listen to the birds in the trees and the cars
on the street half a block away. If it's a nice day
and she's sleeping, or reading, he might

walk around the block, or follow the path
along the river
to where he can see the tide come in,
in waves that might or might not
disappoint his eyes. An afternoon rest,

when it's his turn to lie down, is a kind of
hiding place,
with her promise not to allow anything
(the phone, somebody at the front door, etc.)
that would interrupt his sleep, the same as when

she rests. Driving to the beach for a swim,
going shopping,
doing daily exercises (naked, with the door
closed), meeting a friend for coffee,
each of these is a kind of hiding place,

where he can be alone, and let his thoughts
and his feelings
work their way to the surface. Hiding places
can also be found in plain sight. The kitchen,
for example, when it's time to get supper,

becomes his space, because she does not have
the desire,
the energy, to do the cooking (or the cleaning up).
She stays away, leaving him to his own devices.

(August 10)

WHEN SHE TALKS LIKE THAT

She forgets that she's been saying
the same thing
for weeks, when she talks like that.
I can't count the number of times

I've heard the same despairing words,
the same wish
to put an end to it, though she doesn't
believe me. When she has enough pills,
she says, she'll swallow them and that

will be that. The heat and humidity
are killing her.
She can't breathe. She sometimes gets
so dizzy, she doesn't leave the house
for fear of falling. Though her words

are not new, they feel new to her,
the same way
the sunset feels new to me, from one day
to the next, as the clouds change shape,
blow this way or that, or dissolve to nothing.

She has no energy. She's never been so tired,
so very tired.
She'd like me to get her into an old people's
home. I'm nothing but a burden to you,
she says. My life has been in vain. I've done

nothing of consequence. People have been
nice to me,
and what have I given in return? Nothing.
I must cling to life, or let go.

(August 17)

BE JOYFUL

She's afraid she won't know when
it's time
to give up the struggle and accept
the fact that she's going to die,

like everyone else. For a long time
she thought
she might be the exception that proves
the rule, the one person who never dies,
but no, apparently not. She's no different

from any other living thing, including
the animals
and the plants, each with its alloted time
on this earth. She's more like them than not,
she tells herself, and finds comfort in the words.

She resists the temptation to despair. Be joyful,
a voice whispers.
Look at what the world still has to offer. Look
at the beauty all around. Listen to the birds
in the trees – the blue jays, the sparrows,

the starlings that come by the hundreds,
and the crows.
Salute the fledglings, erect, alert, and orderly,
marching in single file across the street.
Touch and smell the flowers – the roses,

the nasturtiums, the hydrangea, and the phlox.
Marvel at the way
they grow wild and take over the garden.
Study the stars in the sky – Venus to the west,
Jupiter to the south, Mars, the red planet,

to the east, bright as a lantern, and so many others
as darkness descends.
Remember nights like this, dinners with friends,
the gift of laughter, and what it means to love and be
loved.

(August 24)

UNCOUPLING/COUPLING

Their life, after all these years, is
uncoupling
by the minute and there's nothing
they can do about it, nothing

they *want* to do about it, even if
they could.
To step back from each other,
to take a fresh look at how they've
come to this point, is normal, as is

the fact that some things are now
beyond their capacity.
What seemed important is no longer
important. Sex (though the memory of sex
is still very much alive in their bodies),

travel (though they end up in some
strange places
in their dreams), friends (though some friends
have made the effort to stay in touch),
concerts, movies, poetry readings,

walks in nature – none of these is
so pressing
that it has to be attended to right away,
or anytime soon (or ever), though once upon
a time that was the feeling. But for every

uncoupling, every step back, there is
a new coupling,
a new way of being together, for example,
the practice of holding each other, mornings
and evenings, for long periods of time,

or the ritual of reading to each other from
a favorite book,
or the pleasure of driving to the mountain
to view the lights of the city, or the whim
of stopping at a café where they can talk about

whatever it is they want to talk about.
The old ways
they can let go, like a pocketful of coins
that have become too heavy to carry.

(August 31)

ODE TO DRAGONFLIES

This time, she notices something she didn't notice before,
a dragonfly,
resting on a limb of the tree, its wings stretched horizontally,
perfectly motionless. Where did it come from, so quietly,

so stealthily? An intense green and blue-green in color,
almost metallic,
it has eyes that see in every direction, and it flies
backwards as well as forwards, as it hunts for prey,
mosquitoes mainly, and midges. Try to imagine

the life history of the dragonfly, how
the nymph
(the larval stage) lives under water, feeding
on worms, crustaceans, and even small fish,
for as long as five years. When the time is right,

the skin down the back of the thorax splits,
releasing
the head, the thorax, and the legs of the adult within
the nymph, called the imago. The adult lives a month
or two but does not survive winter. When a dragonfly

lands on someone, it means good luck. It means change
is imminent,
change for the better, rejuvenation after a period of trials
and hardship, hope for the transformation of death
into something that can be accepted, even welcomed.

Years ago, being treated for cancer, she remembers
keeping
a dragonfly pin attached to her turban because,
she believed, she could hear its wings (made of
abalone shells) beating, making a sound

that had a real, if inexplicable healing effect.
Ever since,
the dragonfly has served as emblem for the force
that lifts her up in times of darkness.

                                        (September 7)

A NEW SHIRT

His shirt *is* a little ratty,
it's true,
though there are no holes
in front, or missing buttons,

as happened with his previous
shirt,
and the one before that, only
a little fraying at the edges,
around the collar, at the cuffs,

and along the hem. To her mind
it's important
to dress well at all times in case
someone drops by, unexpectedly,
for a visit, or they decide to go out

for a cup of coffee, or they happen
to run
into a friend, or they decide to take
a drive to see what the city lights
look like in their absence, even though

they don't go out much these days
and people
don't bother very often to look them up
because it's hard to think of something
to talk about, isn't it, when the person

sitting opposite is very ill. If she
fails
to wear her watch, she feels
naked, she says, the same
for her favorite pair of earrings,

from her granddaughter, which she
wears
almost every day. The red and purple
viscose scarf, made in India, matches
and draws out the color of the earrings.

When her shoes start to look
worn,
she buys a new pair, or finds a pair
in her closet, as good as new, which
she had forgot about. She's a beautiful

woman, so why not dress to her own
advantage,
when it makes her feel better about
herself, and about the world in general.
So yes, he will dig into his dresser,

or his closet, to find a new shirt, or one
that's like new,
if it will make her happy and bring
that light to her eyes that he loves.

(September 14)

ACKNOWLEDGMENTS

I owe everything to Elaine Amyot, my wife of 25 years. The poems are about her, and me, during a twelve-month period, September 22, 2017, through to September 14, 2018, a few months before her death from heart failure. She was the first reader of each poem as I brought it forth for her to see. She was my first and most important editor. She did not hesitate to tell me what she liked, what she didn't like, and what failed to move her at all. She was unflinching in her support of my year-long project.

Wesley McNair has always had a good word to say about my writing efforts, a good word that is always at the same time insightful and wise. Recently poet laureate of the state of Maine, Wesley has created a body of work that is recognized as one of the most interesting in America today. I always feel humbled in his presence, especially when he calls me brother and treats me as an equal. More to the point, his poetry is a great inspiration to me for the kind of poetry I would like to write myself.

My friend in Paris, Robert Bubrovszky, whom I met in Toronto in 1982 and with whom I've been in correspondence ever since, by letters back and forth, usually handwritten, every month or two for over 30 years, has always been among the first readers of my poems and my fiction, and has always, with his vast reading and his love of literature, given me insightful and helpful and encouraging comments. He puts what I write in the context of what other writers write.

If I say less about the other people I'm going to mention, it's only because I'm running out of space. Marilyn Lerch and Janet Hammock have been great friends to me in recent years, and Marilyn's poetry has always made me think outside the box. The box, that is, that I box myself into, when I'm not able to see what's happening around me, when it should be plain as day. It was Marilyn, by the way, and Jan too, who led me (by the hand) to Chapel Street Editions and Keith Helmuth.

Special thanks to Colleen Furlotte for her support, not just for my writing, which has been substantial, but for helping me through the dark days that followed Elaine's passing. Thank you to Kimberly Gautreau for her contagious enthusiasm for the importance of poetry and for our meetings to talk about nothing but poetry—and Elaine. Thank you to Ann Millar for being such a good and true friend and taking seriously Elaine's request "Look after Ed."

Thank you to Elizabeth Blanchard for her generosity of spirit, her commitment to the writing life, and most especially for writing the thoughtful Foreword to this book, which tells me a lot about what I was doing, often unknown to myself. Thank you to Keltie Campbell for being a good friend to Elaine and always keen to know what I was writing. The last words I ever heard Elaine speak were "au revoir" to Keltie as she left the hospital room, so faintly that no one heard but me.

Thank you to Heather Steeves, my step-daughter, for being interested in my writing and for making good comments whenever I posted one of my poems on Facebook and for keeping me part of the family. Thank you to Alex, my son, for asking to see my poetry and my fiction, and to Nicole, his wife, for asking me to write a poem for their wedding. Thank you to Danielle Cyr who for many years has taken an interest in my writing, and made me feel the importance of the writing life, irrespective of success in publishing.

Special thanks go out to the Breach House Gang, including Rita Auffrey, Judy Bowman, Herménégilde Chiasson, Elizabeth Blanchard, Zev Bagel, Dave Skyrie, Noeline Bridge, Nancy Schofield, and Roméo Savoie, to whom I first read many of these poems. Thank you to Ray Soucie for talking with me. Thank you to Helene Robb for feeding me—intellectually and actually. There are so many others I might mention, and I hope they will forgive me for not doing so. Finally, though, I must say what a pleasure it has been working with Keith Helmuth and his "team" at Chapel Street Editions. I feel very lucky that our paths have crossed.

ABOUT THE AUTHOR

Edward Lemond has lived in the Moncton, New Brunswick area since 1993. Before that, he lived for 24 years in Halifax, Nova Scotia. He grew up in Long Beach, California and Lafayette, Indiana, and came to Canada in 1969. He was a bookseller for twenty-one years, first in Halifax, then Moncton. Ed was one of the founders of the Frye Festival, co-chair of the Program Committee from the first festival in 2000 through the April, 2011 festival. He started the Attic Owl Reading Series, held monthly in Moncton since August, 1994. He is a novelist and poet, and has recently completed a novel titled *Equal Affection*.

"Renewal"– Elaine Amyot

ABOUT THE ARTIST

Originally from Quebec, Elaine Amyot lived in the Moncton area for almost 50 years. A visual artist, she had more than forty solo exhibitions and participated in more than one hundred group exhibitions. She was a founding member of Galerie Sans Nom and of Galerie 12, both at the Aberdeen Cultural Centre in Moncton. In 1990 she received the medal of the city of Moncton for exceptional services rendered to the community.

In the summer of the year 2000 she coordinated *Présence 27,* an exhibition-installation of women artists at the Galerie d'Art de l'Université de Moncton. In 2010 she published her first book, *The Seven Gates: A Memoir of a Descent*, illustrated with many of her own works of art. In August of 2015 she was godmother (marraine) of la Folie des Arts at the Centre des arts et de la culture in Bouctouche, N. B. During this festival she had a solo exhibition titled "A Fierce Energy." The work on the cover of this book, titled "Male Mothering," was part of this exhibition. Elaine was a proud mentor of several young women writers and artists. She died February 27, 2019, at age 86.

www.ingramcontent.com/pod-product-compliance
Lightning Source LLC
Chambersburg PA
CBHW071246070526
44583CB00017B/2352